Anonymous

Constitutions of the Third Order Regular of the Sisters of

Saint Francis of the Immaculate Conception

Anonymous

Constitutions of the Third Order Regular of the Sisters of Saint Francis of the Immaculate Conception

ISBN/EAN: 9783337340377

Printed in Europe, USA, Canada, Australia, Japan

Cover: Foto ©Lupo / pixelio.de

More available books at **www.hansebooks.com**

CONSTITUTIONS

OF THE

THIRD ORDER REGULAR

OF THE

Sisters of Saint Francis,

OF THE

IMMACULATE CONCEPTION.

LITTLE FALLS, MINN.

1893.
NORDSTERN PRINT, ST. CLOUD.

⟶⋇⟵

BLESSING OF OUR
HOLY FATHER, SAINT FRANCIS.

Whosoever shall observe these Rules, shall be blessed in Heaven by the heavenly Father, on earth by His beloved Son, and by the Holy Spirit, the Paraclete, and by all the Angels and Saints. And I, Brother Francis, your humble servant, confirm as far as I can for all eternity, this most holy Blessing. AMEN!

⟶⋇⟵

CURSE OF SAINT FRANCIS

Against Those Who Lead a Scandalous Life.

By Thee, most Holy Father, by the whole Celestial Court, and by me, the poorest of all, be cursed, who by their bad example, spoil and destroy what Thou didst build up, and dost not cease to build up, by Holy Brethren of this Order. Amen.

"It is a dreadful thing to fall into the hands of the living God."- Heb. x., 31.

On the End of this Community.

Divine Mercy has called us to a Community that has a Two-fold End: The first and most important is our own Sanctification, the second, the Education and Training of Youth in Parochial Schools and Academies. The first End is obtained by faithfully observing the simple and perpetual vows of poverty of chastity and obedience, according to the Rule of the Third Order of St. Francis, as approved by his Holiness, Pope Leo X. for religious of both sexes. The second End will be obtained by observing the general rules of Christian instruction.

The following constitutions are put down to help the the Sisters obtain both Ends. They define the obligations imposed upon them by the holy Rule, and serve at the same time as a guide in the practice of virtues peculiar to a religious life.

CHAPTER I.

RECEPTION OF NOVICES.

§ 1. RECEPTION.

1. Those that desire admittance into the Community must have the qualities prescribed by the holy Rule, must descend from a lawful marriage, enjoy a good reputation, possess a sound judgment and a tractable character, and have the vocation of a religious life.

2. They must not be afflicted with any defects of the body, inward diseases or outward deformities, whereby they would become unfit for the life in the Community, or disagreeable to others. No Postulant will be received as long as her parents really need her help.

3. They must be free from debts and other civil obligations, and, as a rule, not be younger than fifteen years nor older than thirty. They ought to present certificates of their baptisms. They must also have received the Sacraments of Confirmation.

4. Persons that wore the habit of any other community are not easily to be admitted. The reason why they left ought to be cautiously investigated, and the conviction obtained that they will accustom themselves in the Community to the life after the Spirit of St. Francis.

5. Postulants can be admitted by the Mother Superior only, who will look in this important affair, more at the supernatural calling and good qualities of the Postulant than at her dowry. The dowry has to be fixed according to the decision of the Council of the Mother Superior.

6. Should the Postulant have too great obstacles in approaching the Mother Superior, any Sister Superior of a Mission may be commissioned by the Mother Superior to examine such a Postulant. A faithful report of such an examination must be sent to the Mother Superior, who will decide regarding the admittance of such a Postulant.

7. Only from the day of Profession the Community has a claim to the dowry during the Postulate and the Novitiate, the expenses of boarding and of necessary clothing only can be asked.

§ 2. POSTULATE.

1. The Postulant, having been admitted, will be sent by the Mother Superior to the home of Novices, where she will stay during her Postulate under the direction of the Mistress of Novices, or of that of the Mistress of Postulants. She will make the exercises of the Community, except recitation of divine office, with the Novices. Her apparel ought to be plain and uniform; As black dress with a cape, purple veil, black cap with white ruffle.

2 The Postulate lasts six months. It may, however, (for sufficient reasons,) be shortened or prolonged by the Mother Superior.

3. In case the Sisters Superior of the house of Novices, with the assisstants, should be convinced of a Postulant's not being fit for a religious life, they will notify the Superior of it, who will then dismiss the Postulant. Ten days before the end of the Postulate, the votes have to be taken of all the perpetual professed sisters of the Mother House, for each postulant; and the postulant if admitted to the habit, will ask for it in the usual way.

§ 3. RECEPTION.

1. The Reception takes place by the Bishop of the diocese, or his Delegate, according to the Ceremony of the Community.

2. The habit of the Novices consits of a coarse woolen dress of a brownish color, a scapular, a brown mantle, a white coif and guimpe, a white veil, and a woolen, knotted cord. The white veil may be replaced by a black veil on Missions where the sisters have to go to services in the parochial church, and where the Novices teach in parochial schools.

§ 4. Novitiate.

1. The Novitiate lasts two years. During this time the Novices must be well educated and instructed.

2. They are under the direction of the Mistress of Novices; they owe to her love, obedience, and candidness.

3. In order to leave them full liberty concerning their vocation, they are allowed, twice or three times a year, to converse alone with their nearest relatives or their guardians. At other times they are only allowed

to converse with strangers in presence of a Professed Sister.

4. The Novices must be separated from the Professed Sisters, except in the refectory and in the choir. They will not hold an office that could hinder them in their spiritual exercises. Yet, the Sisters Superior may appoint them, with the consent of the Mistress of Novices, to help Professed Sisters, or the Mistress of Novices may do the same, with the Sister Superior's permission.

5. Without real necessity, no Novice can be sent on a Mission. The necessity has to be considered by the Mother Superior, and by her Council.

6. During her stay on the Mission, the Novice is under the direction of the Sister Superior of the Mission, who has to see that the work does not extinguish in the Novice the spirit of devotion and of prayer, according to the admonition of our Holy Father, St. Francis.

7. At the end of six months after the reception, the Sister Superior of the Novitiate investigates the conduct of the Novices. For this end every perpetual— Professed Sister of the Mother House, appears before the Sister Superior, to tell frankly the faults and imperfections noticed in the Novices. The result of this investigation is to be reported to the Mother Superior.

8. In case the Sister Superior, her two Assistants, and the Mistress of Novices, agree concerning a Novice as not showing a religious calling, they will notify the Mother Superior of it. The Mother Superior with her assistants, will then deside whether such a Novice be

dismissed or for further probation retained. Novices whose calling remains doubtful must not easily be admitted to Profession. The virtues of the Novice ought to be, rather than their other good qualities, the reason why she is admitted.

9. At the end of the twelfth month of the Novitiate, the second investigation takes place; the last two months before profession.

10. Within eight days following the last investigation, the votes of admission or dismission must be collected, not only in the Novitiate, but also on those Missions where the Novices were dwelling longer than two months.

11. The Perpetual Professed Sisters only are allowed to vote, and then only those who were, previous to the voting, living for two months in the some house with the Novice. The voting itself is done by white and black ballots. Care has to be taken that no natural motives influence the voting. Natural liking or disliking must be put aside in this important affair. If one does not vote according to her own conscience she may aggravate it, may do injustice to the Novice and to the Community, and may hely causing many sins and scandals.

12. In case the Novice receives two thirds of the votes, she will be admitted, if she has more than half against her, she will be dismissed without delay; if she has more than one-third, against her, the vocation is considered doubtful, and the Mother Superior with her assistants has to decide it.

13. One month, at least, before Profession, the Sister Superior will petition the Bishop of the diocese, if

and when it pleases his Grace, to perform the canonical examination.

14. The Novice who is to be admitted to take the vows must, in the usual way, petition the Sisters when assembled in Chapter; she has also to make a spiritual retreat before Profession.

N. B. Those Sisters who are admitted to Perpetual Profession will, in time, dispose of their temporal affairs.

CHAPTER II.

PROFESSION AND VOWS.

1. The year of probation having expired, the Sisters take the simple Vows of Poverty, of Chastity and of obedience for three years.

2. This Profession takes place before the Bishop of the diocese or his Delegate in the Chapel of the Novitiate, according to the Ceremonial of this Community.

FORMULA OF PROFESSION.

3. I, Sister N. N., vow and promise to Almighty God, to the Blessed Mary, ever Virgin, to our Holy Father, St. Francis, to all the Saints in Heaven, to you, Rev. Father, and to you Ven. Mother, to live for the salvation of my soul, all the days of my life, (or, for three years) in Poverty, in Chastity, and in Obedience, according to the Rule approved by his Holiness, Leo X., for Members of the Third Order of St. Francis, living in Community. I also promise to observe the Constitutions of the Franciscan Sisters of the Immaculate Conception, of the diocese of St. Cloud, approved by his Grace, the Bishop of said Diocese.

4. The dress of the Professed Sisters consists of a coarse, woolen habit of brownish color, of a white woolen cord with three knots, of a brown scapular, of a brown mantle four inches from the ground.

Double bandeau, linen guimpers, muslin cap and double thin veil for the streets. They wear ordinary shoes and may at home, wear slippers of common stuff, without embroidery; In places where it is needed, they will also, outside, wear overshoes. They moreover wear, from the time of temporary Profession, a crucifix outside with black string, to be continually reminded of Christ crucified. The Perpetual Professed receive a ring as a singn of their perpetual union with Christ. The Sisters on Missions will, for uniformity's sake, endeavor to follow the Mother House in respect to the quality, the color, and the cut of the habit and of the whole attire.

§ 1. POVERTY

1 The administration and the use of their own property is altogether forbidden to the Professed Sisters. They must therefore dispose of their property (the dowry excepted) before Perpetual Profession. They are allowed to consult upon disposing of their property with God fearing and prudent persons. At the same time they must also dispose of the property that might fall to them in future. Whatever and howsoever they dispose of their property, they should always make this proviso, that in case they are dismissed or have to leave the Community according to a decision of the lawful spiritual authority (which God forbid) they can enter again into the full possession of their property.

2. After the Sisters have done so, they will be free from every earthly care and follow the example of our Holy Father St. Francis who selected Poverty for Jesus sake as his spouse and inheritance. The virtue of Poverty they ought to esteem and love highly and consider it the foundation and ornament of the Community. Poverty must even follow them into the grave In death Poverty must not be denied whilst it was practiced during life. Ordinary coffins should enclose their mortal remains; pomp and wordly show should be far away frow their funerals. Unnecessary expenses must not be made.

3. Through the virtue of Poverty the Sisters bind themselves to a perfect common mode of life, uniformity must be observed in all, there ought to be no distinction in dress, in dwelling and in the other necessaries of life. Every House must therefore supply its members with the necessary things.

4. In every thing must appear uniformity and simplicety. The Houses must be plain and suitable in their arrangements.

5. There ought to be nothing in the cells save a washstaud, a bedstead with an appropriate bed, a chair, a crucifix, and a few books and pictures. No table? *ju*)

6. No Sister is permitted to keep for her use, in her cell, anything locked, as money, eatables, etc., no one must withdraw anything from the sight of the Sister Superior.

7. Without permission of the Sister Superior, no donations must be made or received by the Sisters; in likewise, nothing be loaned or borrowed.

8. The clothing that are daily used, are left to each one for her use; the rest are kept in a common wardrobe.

9. The necessary linens are given to each Sister on a certain day.

10. Books and stationeries are kept for the common usage in a separate room.

11. The Sisters ought to be careful and economical in every thing entrusted to their charge, so that nothing be lost or damaged through their fault, but, on the contrary, everything be used as long as possible.

12. Sisters sent to another House are only allowed to take along their breviary, and their own manuscripts, except the Sister Superior permits more.

13. Poverty, however should not prevent the Sisters to preserve the greatest cleanliness, not only in the Convent and in the chapel, but also in the cells, and in clothing, and in house furniture, as it is becomming a Spouse of Jesus Christ.

§ 2. Chastity.

1. The Vow of Chastity obliges the Sisters to avoid everything in thoughts, words and deeds that is contrary to this holy virtue.

2. But, as Chastity is a duty of every Christian, a Sister, sinning against this beautiful virtue, would commit a double sin, one against the holy Vow, the other against the virtue of Chastity.

3. All religious Communities pay a great deal of attention to the practice of this virtue; how much more must not a community, which has its special end placed in educating youth and leading it in the practice of virtue, esteem it and endeavor to preserve it.

4. To keep this virtue with the utmost fidelity, the Sisters must, with the greatest care, guard their senses and conscientiously observe the rules of religious modesty.

5. Their conversing with each other must be accompanied with the greatest respect toward each other and with decency. Only completely dressed ought the Sisters to appear before their fellow Sisters. Caresses amongst themselves and to children must by all means be avoided.

6. No Sister is allowed to enter the cell of another Sister without permission of the Sister Superior; not even the bed department of another Sister. The beds in the common dormitory must be separated in a becomming way by curtains.

Correspondence, Visits, Parlor etc?

7. The Sisters must close their hearts against every affection that is solely natural and flee all sensual friendships. In doubts they ought to have, with the greatest open-heartedness and candidness, recourse to the Father Confessor.

§ 3. OBEDIENCE.

1. Through the Vow of obedience, the Sisters renounce their own will. In virtue of this Vow they are bound to obey their Superior in everything that is not (plainly) a sin (and against the rule?)

2. The Sisters must consider their Superiors as persons that hold God's place, and must submit to their orders without delay, without disatisfaction, without inward or outward murmurings; with love, respect, cheerfulness and simplicity.

3. As peace and success of every House, in particular, and of the whole Community, at large, depend principally upon the perfect observance of this Vow, every Sister that acts grievously and publicly against Obedience, or against respect due to the Superior, may be punished by kneeling, at the common meal (dinner or supper) on the floor, and by partaking only of bread and water, and by being excluded from recreation for one or several days.

CHAPTER III.

EXERCISES OF PENANCE.

1. The Sisters are members of an order that follows a Life of Penance. They ought, therefore, continually to be animated with the Spirit of Penance, and keep it before themselves as a motive of action in their spiritual exercises, in their works, in all their deeds and omissions.

2. This Spirit of Penance must encourage every Sister, not only to the practices of Penance and all hardships of religious life, but even to accept cheerfully all troubles and ever so difficult duties in the service of the neighbors. She should even, considering her own sins and the love of Jesus Christ towards mankind, rejoice at the occassion of practicing the Spirit of Penance of self denial.

§ 1. Fasts and Abstinence.

1. A dispensation in regard to the Fasts prescribed in the Rule has been given in consideration of the continuing and fatiguing work in the schools and at home. The Sisters will therefore observe the Fasts of the

Church and the following days of Fasts and of Abstinence.

a. Every Friday in the year, except Christmas; Assumption, Immaculate Conception and the feast of St.
Francis.

b. Vigil day of the Feast of St. Francis.

c. Day of Abstinence is every Saturday.

2. The Sister Superior of every House has the power
to dispense the Sisters under her charge in fasting and
abstaining, in case The Sisters are weakly or sickly or
burdened by hard work. The Sister Superior, however,
cannot dispense in the days prescribed by the Church.

3. Sisters traveling follow the rules of the diocese.

§ 2. CHAPTER OF FAULTS.

1. To prevent transgressions of the holy Rule and to
practice continually humility, the foundation of all virtues, the Chapter of Faults takes place once every week.
The Sisters accuse themselves of all public transgressions of the holy Rule and Customs of the Community.

Faults and imperfections that did not appear in public must not be manifested in the Chapter. This Chapter takes place according to the Ceremonial.

2. The Sister Superior has the right of demanding
the Sisters to accuse themselves publicly, outside of
the Chapter of their public Faults.

3. The Sisters must cheerfully accept in the Spirit
of Penance, the reprimands and humiliations, connec-
ted with this self accusation. They must not excuse or
justify themselves in the Chapter.

Above all, things that happened in the Chapter of

Faults must not become a topic of talk amongst the Sisters.

4. Extra practices of Penance are only allowed with the permission of the respective Superior.

5. Interior mortifications are more important than exterior.

The practice of Humility and Obedience is, in preference to all others, recommended to the Sisters.

6. The Sisters wear their hair cut short.

§ 4. WORKING.

1. The Sisters must perform their work with a holy zeal and with a pure intention; the most insignificant and menial offices must be to them the most liked.

2. The teachers especially should, as they are away from the domestic work on account of their teaching, when time and opportunity allow it, offer themselves to such work as is apt to keep them in humility.

3. No Sister must interfere with the affairs of another over whom she has no authority; but each one be rather diligent in doing well what duty and obedience impose upon her. Nevertheless every Sister should show readiness in helping her fellow Sisters, whenever love requires it.

CHAPTER IV.

DIVINE OFFICE AND PRAYERS.

1. A religious person finds only in Prayer and in interior union with God the necessary strenght to advance in the way of perfection and to work with success, for the salvation of others. Likewise, she finds there consolation and comfort so necessary in carrying,

with joy, the crosses and the sufferings attached to this state of life. The Sisters must, therefore, perform the Spiritual Exercises prescribed with the greatest fidelity and punctuality.

2. They ought, at the first signal of the bell to repair to the spiritual Exercises of the Community.

§ 1. MORNING AND EVENING PRAYERS - GRACE AT MEALS.

1. The Sisters perform the Morning and Evening Prayers and say Grace at Meals, as prescribed by the Ceremonial.

§ 2. CHOIR.

1. A very ancient custom, confirmed by old Constitutions of the Order, granted to female Communities of the Third Order, on account of the outward activity of the Order, the liberty of satisfying the duty to say the Divine Office by reciting the "Officium Marianum". Consequently, the Sisters who can read Latin say daily, instead of the "Breviary Proper," the Officium Marianum," in Latin.

2. The office is said in common wherever it can possibly be done.

3. The Sisters who do the domestic work say for Matins and Lauds twelve Pater and Gloria; for every little hour, seven Pater and Gloria; at the beginning of Prime and Complin, they add the Credo and the Psalm "Miserere." Those that cannot recite the Psalm "Miserere" say three Pater instead of it. They are not obliged to add the Ave Maria; yet it is meritorious, and is usually done.

4. The Sister Superior can dispense with these prayers for Sisters who are prevented by sickness.

§ 3. Meditation and Spiritual Reading.

1. Every morning before Mass, the Sisters spend half an hour in Meditation.

2. In the afternoon another Meditation takes place, provided there is no other Spiritual Exercise instead of it.

3. The Sisters that are hindered from being present at the common Meditation will do it at the time appointed by the Sister Superior.

4. Spiritual Reading takes place at breakfast, dinner and supper. At breakfast one of Thomas a Kempis; at dinner, one of the lives of the Saints: at supper, one of a book that treats of religious life. The Mother Superior may designate the books to be read at dinner and at supper. Perfect silence ought to be observed during the reading; all ought to listen attentively and keep their eyes cast down; those that wait on the Community will be careful, in going to and fro, not to cause any unecessary noise.

§ 4. Examination of Conscience.

Two Examinations of Conscience take place every day. The particular, immediately before dinner; the other at night prayers.

§ 5. Confession and General Absolution.

1. Once every week the Sisters go to Confession; the rank of the Sisters should be well observed in going.

2. Four times a year they appear before the extraordinary Confessor, either to confess, or to receive an exhortation, or his blessing.

3. Both Confessors must be appointed by the Bishop of the diocese.

4. Without weighty reasons a Sister Superior ought not to hinder a Sister in approaching Confession at an unusual time, should such a Sister wish to confess to the ordinary or to the extraordinary Confessor. The Sister Superior will act with due precaution in this case.

5. Weekly confession must be considered as an important means to conquer evil inclination and advance in virtues; the Sisters ought, therefore, prepare themselves conscientiously, yet without anxiety. The Confessions should be humble, sorrowful, candid, plain and short.

6. Confession, itself, and the Father Confessor, as such, must never be the topic of conversation amongst the Sisters. The Sister Superior will see that General Absolution be given on the days appointed in the Ceremonial.

The Father Confessor is Authorized to give it.

§ 6. COMMUNION.

1. The Sisters receive holy Communion the following days:

a. Every Sunday, Tuesday, Thursday and Saturday; on Festivals of the Order with plenary indulgence, and on every first Friday of the month. If there is an extraordinary Communion during the week, Thursday should be omitted. And the Sisters could also receive holy Communion on the day of their Patron Saints.

b. Circumcision of our Lord (Jan. 1); Epiphany of

our Lord (Jan. 6); Feast of the Triumph of the Holy
Name of Jesus (Jan. 14); Purification of the Blessed
Virgin (Feb. 2); St. Joseph (March 19); Annunica-
tion of the Blessed Virgin (March 25); St. Raphael
(April 16); Renewal of Vows; St. John the Baptist
(June 24); St. Peter and St. Paul (June 29); Visita-
tion of the Blessed Virgin (July 2); Dedication of all
the Churches of three Orders of St. Francis (July 4);
Assumption of the Blessed Virgin Mary (Aug. 15);
Nativity of the B. V. (Sept. 8); All Saints day and all
Souls day (Nov 1 & 2); Immaculate Conception of the B.
V. (Dec. 8): Feast of St. Stephen (Dec. 26); Feast of
the Holy Innocents (Dec. 28).

c. Easter Monday; Ascension Day of our Lord;
Penticost Monday; Corpus Christi; Feast of the Sacred Heart of Jesus; Nativity of our Lord.

2. In case a Sister had committed a grievous and
public fault, the Sister Superior would be obliged to re-
mind her of the obligation of omitting holy Communion. The rest the Sister Superior leaves to the judgment of the Father Confessor.

3. Should a Sister omit holy Communion frequently and cause thereby scandal to the other Sisters, her
Sister Superior will notify the Mother Superior of it.

4. In case a Sister is prevented from receiving holy
Communion on the days mentioned, she may, with the
permission of her Sister Superior, approach on other
days of the same week.

§ 7. Holy Sacrifice of Mass.—Visits to The Blessed Sacrament.

1. The Sisters assist daily, with proper attention and devotion, at the holy Sacrifice of Mass.

2. After grace at dinner they repair to the Chapel, reciting the "Miserere"; Perform the Prayer of the Cross (6 Pater, Ave. and Gloria) to gain the indulgence granted to this devotion.

3. The Sisters are advised to visit the Blessed Sacrament sometimes during the day; these visits, however, must not last too long.

§ 8. Silence.

1. Silence has always to be observed in the Chapel in the cells, and in the halls.

2. Silence begins in the evening at the signal given with the bell, and lasts till the hour of Recreation the following day; at noon. Recreation lasts after dinner till 1:30 P. M.; After Supper, Recreation lasts from 7 to 8, P. M.

3. During silence it is allowed to speak about things that do not admit delay; yet it ought to be done in a low tone of voice.

4. The Sisters are also allowed to speak to the Superior about the things that are needed; inquiries that are not urgent ought to be postponed to the appointed time.

The Sisters are allowed to speak to strangers, servants and laborers only with the permission of the Sister Superior. Whenever they are unexpectedly accosted, they should answer shortly, but politely.

§ 9. Annual and Monthly Retreats.

1. As it is absolutely necessary for a religious person to revive and renew frequently the Spirit of Vocation, the Sisters keep one day of every month for Spiritual Exercises.

2. For the same purpose the Sisters make once a year a Retreat at the time appointed by the Mother Superior, (by a Priest approved).

§ 10. Renewal of Vows.

(As customary with all the children of Blessed Francis), the holy Vows are renewed in the manner prescribed by the Ceremonial of the Community, on the 16. of April.

CHAPTER V.

OFFICES AND ELECTIONS.

According to the regulations of the first chapter of the Rule, the Sisters must show a filial respect and a perfect obedience towards the Holy Father, the Pope, and towards the holy Roman Church.

2. Religious Communities are under the Jurisdiction of the Bishop of the diocese, according to the laws of the Church and of the Apostolic Constitutions.

3. Pursuant to the spirit of the Constitution of Benedict XIII., (Paterna Sedis, Dec. 10, 1725,) the Sisters as children of St. Francis, acknowledge and honor the Minister General of the whole Order of Friars Minor as the successor of their Seraphic Father and Founder.

4. For the same reason it is becoming that the Mother Superior asks of the respective Bishop that,

from time to time, a Friar Minor holds conferences, etc., for the Sisters, that in this way the spirit of the Franciscan Order may remain in the Community.

ARTICLE 1.

OFFICES.

DUTIES OF SUPERIORS.

1. The Superiors must not be arrogant on account of their offices, but be foremost in striving after true humility; they ought, therefore, embrace every occassion of humiliating themselves as far as the dignity and respect of their Offices permit it.

2. The are obliged to edify their inferiors in everything, and must avoid, therefore, singularity in nourishment, clothing and furniture; their virtues shall be the only thing wherein they excel.

3. The Superiors must always remember that they are responsible for all that God has entrusted to their care; they must, consequently, watch that the Sisters keep punctually the holy Vows, the Rule and the Constitutions; advance in perfection, faithfully comply with the duties imposed upon them, and that there always reign amongst them unity and charity.

4. The Superiors, considering themselves as Mothers, ought to assist, in great care, the Sisters, as their daughters, in all their corporal and spiritual needs. The love of the Superiors must be kind, i. e., it must bear with the imperfections of the Sisters and offer to them exortation and consolation; their love must be benevolent, and, as such, move them to grant to their inferiors everything that is necessary to their situation,

and to comply with every thing that is not against the Constitutions and the Customs, and that would not be a cause of relaxation; their love must be friendly and obliging, so that it moves the Sisters to candidness and open-heartedness, it must be meek, i. e., the Supeperiors must receive the Sisters at any time, must not treat them harshly and repulsively, but always tell them in a friendly and kind way what they have to do. Finally, the love of the Superiors must be universal, without partiality. If the Superiors be animated with such a love, the Sisters will obey with love and not with fear, and will, with full confidence, have recourse for help to the Superior in everything that troubles them.

5. Yet the love of the Superiors must not degenerate into blind compliancy and into laxity that connives at everything; nor must it weaken discipline. In case the honor of God and the observance of the Constitutions are concerned, the Superiors must unite firmness and meekness, aim to do their duty, and leave the rest to God.

6. They must at transgressons reprimand their inferiors, not with vehemence, but with love; and, if neessary, dictate to them works of mortification and of penance that correspond with the gravity of the transgression.

7. The Sister Superior must notify the Mother Superior of serious transgressions that occurred.

8. The Superiors are bound to keep strict secrecy concerning the things revealed to them; and although being very prudent through experience, they must not confide in their own ability and prudence, but have, in

all humility and confidence, recourse to God, ask Him for light and necessary grace, and, in all affairs and undertakings of importance, and perhaps of important consequences, will ask counsel at a proper place.

§ 2. Mother Superior· – Her Assistants.

1. The government of the Community is entrusted to the Mother Superior, who is elected by the Chapter for the space of three years. This Chapter is composed of all perpetual professed Sisters.

2. The Mother Superior has her residence in the Mother House at Little Falls, Minn., and cannot remove it into any other House of the Community, except with the consent of her Assistants and the Right Rev. Bishop of the diocese.

3. If the Mother House is under the direction of a Sister Superior, the Mother Superior is empowered to interfere with the direction of this House as well as with that of other Houses.

4. The Mother Superior ought, every year, either personally or by one of her assistants delegated by her, to visit the other Houses and remain there some time at such visits.

5. She ought to see whether the regulations are observed and whether care is taken for the corporal and spiritual welfare of the Sisters.

6. It is her duty to depose Superiors that discharge the duties of their offices in a way detrimental to the welfare of the inferiors and to the Community.

7. The Sisters Superiors, as well as the other Sisters, must, as far as possible, endeavor to lighten the

Mother Superiors important trust, given to her by Divine Providence; they must frequently pray for her, subject themselves to her will with filial confidence, and assist her with all their power.

8. Four Assistants constitute the Council of the Mother Superior. They are likewise elected in the Chapter for the term of three years.

The Mother Superior must hold a meeting of the Council regularly once in three months. Moreover she must call a meeting of them in all important affairs that do not admit delay, and in all cases that grant to the Assistants a decisive vote.

The Mother Superior presides and proposes the affairs to be discussed. Before the meeting adjourns she has to ask her Assistants whether they have any remarks to make, and, in case they have, she must receive them with kindness.

9. The Assistants have a decisive vote in the following cases:

a. Whenever a new Mission is to be accepted, or an old one deserted.

b. Whenever a Novice has to be dismissed during the Novitiate before the Community has given their votes.

c. Whenever an incorrigible Sister has to be expelled from the Community. In this case the desision has to be approved by the respective Bishop.

d. Whenever a Sister Superior or the Mistress of Novices is to be elected or deposed. Should, however, the Mother Superior, when visiting a House, find an immediate deposing or removing of a Superior necessary, she need not wait for the consent of the Council, yet she is obliged to give, at the next meeting of the Council, an account of her proceeding and of the reasons that urged her thus to act.

e. Whenever important buying or selling is to be done and when large expenses for building have to be made. Extra ordinary expenses of selling and buying are those that exceed two hundred dollars.

10. New Houses can only be erected with the consent of the Bishop of the Diocese. In like manner, no House must be deserted without having notified the Bishop of the Diocese. In places where the Rule can, in all probability, not be observed, no Houses must be accepted.

11. The Mother Superior and her Council must take care that expenses for building be made only when they are really necessary and that, in buildings to be erected, plainness and propriety be observed.

12. At the election of a Sister Superior, the Mother Superior proposes one Sister for the vacant office, after a consultation with her assistants has taken place. The voting itself is done by white and black ballots. In case the proposed Sister is not elected, the Mother Superior proposes another one.

A Sister who was not accepted for one house may be proposed for another. The election of the Mistress of Novices is done in the same way. But, when the Council has to elect an assistant, it is done by shedule, without any proposal on the part of the Mother Superior.

13. The Assistants are bound to give their opinion frankly and openly, without respect of persons, only ac-

cording to their own Consciences, but with due deference, in all cases, when asked for advice.

14. At a diversity of opinions in the Council, the majority of votes decides, and those members, that constitute minority must acquiesce. At an equality of votes the Mother Superior decides.

•15. Important decisions of the Council must be recorded and signed by those members of the Council that are present.

16. The members of the Council must observe the strictest silence concerning the things that were entrusted to them and not converse about them amongst themselves after the Council. In case decisions have to be published, it is the business of the Mother Superior to do it.

17. The Assistants must be in every thing a help and support to the Mother Superior; offer a helping hand in all occuring affairs; accept willingly every commission; and rejoice in lightening as far as possible, the heavy burden of the Mother Superior.

18. They must not assume any other authority in the Community save the one given them by the Constitutions or by the Mother Superior.

19. In case the Assistants are in a Mission House they must not interfere any further in the direction of the House than the Mother Superior has commissioned them. Yet they will notify the Mother Superior of serious transgressions or abuses which (what God forbid) might have happened.

20. The Mother Superior selects one of her Assistants to be Treasurer and Secretary; she may change

her if she thinks it fit. This Sister is commissioned under the direction of the Mother Superior, with the administration of the temporal affairs of the Community She administers every thing that belongs to the Common Treasury; she audits the account sent, by the Sisters Superiors, to the Mother Superior every third month; she keeps an abstract of the resources and liabilities of each House; she keeps an account of the dowries paid or expected to be paid in future.

21. The Treasurer presents her books, four times a year, to the other Assistants for inspection, after they have, with the Mother Superior, examined the Treasury.

22. The property belongs to the Community in Common. The Mother Superior will see that the titles, deeds, etc., be made according to the laws of the Country. The dowries enter the common Treasury.

23. The Archives must contain the papers and documents that belong to the whole Community, and duplicates of the documents and of the important papers of the Mission Houses. They are in trust of the Secretary of the Mother Superior. The Secretary keeps a catalogue of the Novices, Professed Sisters, and Sisters deceased; she records carefully every thing that refers to the history of the Community; She keeps likewise a list whereby it may easily be found in which House of the Community every Sister is dwelling; she is also ordered to mark down the transactions of the Council.

§ 3. Sister Superior and Her Assistants.

1. All the members of the Houses must consider their Sisters Superiors as their spiritual mothers, sincerly love, honor and respect them.

2. The Sister Superior is not allowed to make remarkable changes in the House without the permission of the Mother Superior. She is particularly not permitted to accept a new field of labor without the knowledge of the Mother Superior.

3. The Sister Superior must take care that the Annals and Inventory of the House be kept in good order and be continued; that expenditures and receipts be well noted, and the archives well guarded.

4. She must every third month, viz; 1st of January, 1st of April, 1st of July, and 1st of October, send a faithful report to the Mother Superior, concerning the spiritual and temporal affairs of the House, as also one concerning the conduct of the Sisters. To this report has to be added an account of the expenditures and receipts of the House, countersigned by her Assistants.

5. One day of every month is to be appointed for the Sisters to go to the Sister Superior to tell to her their needs, be these needs corporal or spiritual. The whole day after the monthly retreat is well adapted for this.

6. In Mission Houses of at least twelve Sisters, the Sister Superior has two Assistants, or consellors; in houses of less than twelve Sisters, there is only one Assistant to the Superior, appointed by the Mother Superior.

7. The Council Sisters of the Houses are nominated by the Mother Superior, who may, if she deems it necessary, appoint one of them Treasurer to the Sister Superior. In case of sickness or absence of the Sister

Superior the Assistant takes her place; and where there are two, the first; if she be also hindered, the second.

8. The Superior must consult their Assistants in all important affairs, and, at least once a month, have with them a private consultation concerning the welfare of the Convent; must show to them, every third month, the books of expenditures and of receipts, as also the Treasury.

9. The Assistants must frankly state their opinion and remember that they violate their duty, if, from human respect, they omit remarks they deem useful. Yet they must be unpretending and prudent, and keep the things entrusted to them secret. Outside of the Council they must not speak about them.

10. At all extra expenses that exceed the sum of twenty five dollars, they have a decisive vote.

11. The Sister Superior, with her Council, is only authorized, to make extra expenses that do not exceed thirty dollars.

12. Should the Assistants perceive serious transgressions or abuses in the House, they are obliged to notify the Sister Superior of it; yet they must not show dissatisfaction in case she does not act according to their opinion. In a case, however, where it would appear to them that the peace and welfare of the House were endangered by the proceedings of the Sister Superior, it will be their duty to notify the Mother Superior of the affair; this, however, must be done with candidness and impartiality. This report can be sent without the knowledge of the Sister Superior.

13. The Assistants have no other authority save that

given to them by the Constitutions and by their Superior. They must always act towards her very respect-
fully and harmoniously; subject themselves humbly to
her will, and be a model to the other Sisters by punctuality observing the holy Rule and Customs of the Community.

§ 4. MISTRESS OF NOVICES.

1. The direction and instruction of the Novices is
wholly and solely entrusted to the Mistress of the Novices; she ought to be at least thirty years old and be
a Perpetual Professed Sister for three years.

2. She instructs the Novices concerning the spiritual and Religious life, and the duties and advantages
thereof. She explains the holy Vows, the holy Rule,
the Constitutions and the customs of the Community.

3. She must endeaver to teach the Novices to esteem
highly their state of life, and to be thankful to God for
the grace of vocation. She must, moreover, endeaver to
fill them with a love for the interior life, with a taske for
the interior conversation with God, with a zeal for interior and exterior mortifications; teach them how to
guard themselves and how to practice their virtues that
are necessary for a religious life; finally she must teach
and direct them to work in a salutary and God-fearing
way.

4. She ought, therefore, carefully train the Novices
in the exercise of meditating, of praying, of examining
their Consciences, and of all the other practices of devotion, and of all duties that refer to the service of God;
she directs them, as far as possible, in the different
kinds of works they have to do, and watches them there

as in all other exercises; she ought also to be present at their recreations.

5. Every third month the Mistress of Novices sends an exact report to the Mother Superior and to the Sister Superior of the Novitiate. This report embraces the Novices vocation and their character, their virtues and their faults, their progress and their state of health. She must, therefore, endeavor that the Novices show towards her a great open-heartedness. She must try to know each one thoroughly. She will do this, partly through continual, kind, patient, and impartial observation, as also by prudently and cautiously judging the reports made concerning them; partly through kind and parental conversation concerning their interior.

6. Moneys, jewels and secular clothes of the Novice, she gives to the Sister Superior for keeping.

§ 5. Sacristan.

1. The Sacristan, particulary, must excel in reverence towards the sacred articles and towards the Chapel; she ought to endeavor to do the duties of her office with the intention to honor the most holy Sacrament.

2. She must act towards the priests with great respect avoid carefully every familiarity, and speak to them only in the Church and in the Sacristy; whenever it is really necessary; and then only in a low voice.

3. She must keep everything entrusted to her, clean and in good order.

4. The Sacristan must also see that the candles be lit at the proper time, in the Chapel and in the Choir: that the Chapel be locked at the appointed hour, and

that everything necessary for Divine Service be there
in time.

§ 6. PORTRESS.

1. The Portress must comply with the duties of her
office, with religious Modesty, with punctuality, and with
politeness. She must avoid every familiarity towards
strangers, obstain from every impolite question, from
everything that could disturb the Spirit of Recollection.
In opening the Convent entrance, she must not look attentively at things that happen outside.

2. She must faithfully deliver to the Sister Superior
the messages, letters, and packages; she is not allowed
to send anything without the knowledge and the Order
of the Superior.

3. In case the Sister Superior, or the Sisters whom
outsiders whish to see, are in the Choir, or at prayer,
or at table, the Portress will inquire if she shall call
them immediately.

4. Alms, which the Sister Superior gives to her for
the poor, she will distribute with great charity; alms
offered to the Sisters, no matter how small they be,
she accepts with thankfulness.

5. The Portress is not allowed, without permission
of the Superior to entrust her office to any of the Sisters. She must be careful to have the entrance to the
Convent well locked, particularly the outside doors at
night.

§ 7. TEACHER.

1. A Sister who is a Teacher ought frequently to
consider the importance of her office; it indeed afford

her an opportunity, not only of enriching the minds of youth with useful sciences, but moreover of gaining souls for God. She does this by planting in the hearts of the children true virtues which enable them to work out their salvation in all the vicissitudes of life.

2. The office of a Teacher is a true, Apostolate, rich in merits before God and men. A Teacher ought therefore, continually like the Guardian Angel, direct her eyes towards God and on her pupils, and without neglecting her religious duties, work in enducating youth with indefatigable zeal and total self denial. She has to consider well the purpose the Community has in educating youth. These purpose are:

a. To teach the Children the principles of a virtuous life.

b. To teach the children sciences that will really be useful to them in future life.

3. But this end cannot be obtained by instruction alone, good example and divine grace have to help. It is therefore necessary that a Teacher earnestly work at her own perfection in continually walking and always working in the presence of God, keeping up the Spirit of Prayer and Devotion, and faithfully observing her holy Rule and these Constitutions.

4. In the dealings with children, the Teacher should always be full of propriety, earnestness, kindness and Charity. She will avoid too great intimacy with the children, to inspire them with respect as well as with love and confidence. She must never speak to them concerning the defects or faults of her fellow-Sisters, nor about the affairs of the Community.

5. She must be watchful that nothing, which has been known remains unnoticed; yet she must not show suspicion.

6. In everything that refers to the instruction or teaching, she will subject her judgment to that of the Sister Superior; with her as with all the other that instruct, she will converse in perfect peace and union; for mutual Charity and union in action are absolutely necessary.

N. B. The Sisters will endeavor to follow, as far as possible, the same method of teaching and use the same text books in all their schools. The Sisters will not be allowed, as a general rule, to lead choirs, composed of ladies and gentlemen; where only the children sing, they may do it.

ARTICLE II.

Election of the Mother Superior, and of Her Assistants.

1. The Mother Superior calls a Chapter of all the perpetual Professed Sisters every third year in the Month of July or August, for the purpose of electing the Mother Superior and her Assistants; moreover of consulting about the most important affairs of the Community.

2. This Chapter takes place in the Mother House at Little Falls, Minn., in which all the Perpetual Professed Sisters are allowed to vote. The Bishop of St. Cloud presides, assisted by two witnesses, or his Lordship's Delegate with two witnesses.

3. The Mother Superior will at least two months previous announce this Chapter by a circular to all the

Houses, and order some prayers to be said in common by the members of the Houses to implore God's blessing on the Chapter.

On the day of the Chapter itself, all sisters of the Community receive holy Communion, with the same intention.

4. In case one of the Sisters who is entitled to vote cannot be present at the Chapter on account of distance or of business, she will state the reasons to the Mother Superior, who, with her assistants, will dispense with her. Those who are absent cannot vote by proxy or by another Sister.

5. On the day of election there ought to be celebrated a Solemn High Mass. At the close of Mass the Hymn, "Veni Creator" is chanted with the oration, "De Spiritu Sancto," "de Immaculata Conceptione," "de Beato Patre nostro Francisco." After this the Sisters who have an active vote repair at the appointed hour, in procession to the Chapter Hall.

6. The Mother Superior kneels down before the Bishop or His Delegate, and resigns her office into his hands, in the following words:

Right Reverend Father: I resign into your hands my office. I thank all my fellow Sisters for the confidence and the love they have shown to me; and I acknowledge having committed many faults during the administration of my office. May the merciful Lord pardon me and bless our Community."

The Bishop then responds: "The community releases you from your office which you hold as Mother Superior, and may the merciful Lord, the Father, the Son and the Holy Ghost, bless you and your Community. Amen.

7. This being done, every Sister writes on a slip of paper, prepared for that purpose, the name of the Sister for whom she votes; then all approach the Bishop, after their rank of Reception, and place the ticket into the ballot box.

8. Absolute majority of votes decides the election.

9. The Bishop presiding, or his Delegate, mixes and counts the votes in presence of his two witnesses, reads them and presents them, one by one, to everyone of his witnesses, who note them down. The votes having been counted, the Bishop announces the result to the Chapter.

10. The votes will then immediately be burned in the presence of the Chapter, that their contents remain secret.

11. Should the number of votes not correspond with the number of Sisters who had to vote, or should no one obtain an absolute majority, the votes are also burned without delay, and the voting begins anew.

12. Should no absolute majority ensue at the second and at the third voting, the fourth voting begins, but the votes are given only two Sisters who had the highest number of votes. If no majority is obtained for one of them at the first and second balloting, the Bishop or his Delegate decides the Election. If this happens, it has to be recorded.

13. The Members of the Chapter are bound to give their votes to such as they really deem worthy of the offices and able for them. The voting is done secretly and should remain secret:

The Sisters, consequently, should afterwards not say for whom they voted.

14. To follow party spirit is strictly forbidden at every Election; Also intriguing to carry an Election. Whoever will be found guilty of this will be severely punished, and may be deprived of her active and passive vote. Should a Sister, know such doings to be going on, she will be bound to notify the Bishop or his Delegate of it.

15. As Mother Superior, a Sister can be elected who is at least thirty five years, and five years Perpetual Professed; who was moreover, a Member of the Council or a Sister Superior, and always showed a praise worthy conduct in the Community. In case of necessity, however, it will be allowed to elect one of thirty two years and Perpetual Professed for three years provided she possess the other necessary qualities.

16. The Mother Superior is elected for three years and may once be re-elected by a majority of two thirds. After an intervening of three years, she may, in the usual way that is, by absolute majority, be re-elected.

17. In case the Mother Superior dies or resigns, or is legally deposed, the first Assistant succeeds her and another Assistant is elected.

18. A Mother Superior who deems it necessary for the greater honor of God and the welfare of the Community to resign, on account of her feeble health or her age, or from other laudable motives, will propose her reasons to her Assistants, and, if they consent, ask the Bishop to be permitted to resign.

19. For serious reasons only, the Mother Superior

may be removed; these reasons have to be considered by her Assistants and by the Bishop of St. Cloud.

20. Immediately after the election of the Mother Superior, the Assistants are elected in the same way. The same Sister may be re-elected.

21. An Assistant must be thirty years old, or at least twenty eight, and Perpetual-Professed for three years.

22. A Sister who is a full Sister or first cousin of the Mother Superior, cannot be elected as her assistant. Likewise two full Sisters cannot be Asisstants at the same time, nor an aunt and her niece.

23. Only Sisters who are really able and willing to help the Mother Superior, must be elected as her Assistants.

24. At the death of an Assistant, the other Assistance elect a new one by a majority of votes: this Assistant has to resign with the rest at the next Chapter.

25. The proceeding of the Chapter must be approved and signed by the Bishop or his Delegate, then recorded and signed by every Sister of the Chapter and finally signed with the seal of the Community.

26. The Chapter being finished, all the Sisters of the Community repair in procession to the Chapel, where the result of the Chapter is announced and the Chapter declared finished. The "Te Deum" is chanted in thanksgiving.

27. On the same day, or the day after, the Mother Superior calls her Assistants to meet in Council. The other Sisters, where entitled to vote in the Chapter, do not partake in it, yet they are allowed to send in their wishes concerning the Community.

CHAPTER VI.

CONDUCT AT HOME AND ABROAD.

§ 1. SIMPLICITY.

1. Our holy Father St. Francis, was animated with
a true and holy Simplicity, as all his deeds do show; in
the sixth Chapter of the holy Rule, he commends this
holy virtue emphatically. The Sisters therefore, should
try to possess this lovely virtue.

2. Simplicity should, above all appear in filial candidness towards the Sisters Superiors, in charitable
conversations amongst themselves, in kind conduct towards their pupils, and in their dealings with outsiders;
their pupils should be taught to love simplicity,

3. The Convents and Houses should proclaim aloud
that the Sisters esteem the holy virtue of simplicity
and that they carefully guard it.

§ 2. MUTUAL LOVE.

1. Love is the fullfillment of the law; it makes a religious Community a true Paradise; where love rules;
one breaths the sweet odor of Heaven.

2. The Sisters should be of but one heart and one
soul. As they strive after the one and the same end,
namely to serve God, one tie only should unite them
that is a true holy love, a love that is not supported by
natural and human motives, but by God's holy Will.
About this love St. Paul the Apostle says: "Charity is
patient, is kind; Charity envieth not, dealeth not per-
versely; is not provoked with anger; thinketh no evel;

rejoiceth not in iniquity, but rejoiceth with the truth; beareth all things." 1. Cor. XIII, 4, 5, 6, 7.

3. The Sisters will endeavor to help each other in the most charitable way; will embrace every opportunity of showing their affections; will avoid everything that could disturb Mutual Love, and perfect unity. Wherefore they ought to suppress every aversion, and every rash judgment as quick as possible; particularly if such thoughts are against older or presiding Sisters. They must never show the least harshness, excitement or indifference.

4. At removals or travels from one House to another the Sisters must be very careful not to extol one House at the expense of another; nor to reveal defects; they must likewise be careful to avoid expressions against charity by talking about the faults of their fellow Sisters. If this is not carefully avoided, disunion will follow.

No Sister deserves the name of a religious person if she does not, remembering her own weakness, bear with patience and love the imperfections and peculiarities of her fellow Sisters.

5. Every Particular and secret familiarity, every private friendship and inordinate predilection, must be avoided with great care; because if it is not done true charity which must unite all the Sisters will be destroyed. Every Sister Superior is bound to be vigilant regarding this point, and be careful to use appropriate means extirpate private friendships.

6. It is the duty of the Sister Superior to see that every Sister in the Community, who, at arrival or on a

journey enters a House, be received with all charity and be sufficiently provided with everything she needs.

7. Provided one Sister has really offended another she shall immediately, or as soon as possible, in every case before retiring at night, approach her fellow Sister and ask pardon.

The other Sister ought to admit this act, with humility and kindness; she must not speak about the things that happened, nor utter reproaches or reprimands.

§ 3. RECREATION.

1. Recreation serves to relieve the spirit and to make it more fit for the service of God; it cultivates love and many other virtues whenever it is kept in the spirit of obedience and in the proper way.

2. The Sisters must be careful to avoid foolish levity as well as cold disinterestedness; likewise to noisy or worldly amusements, conversations concerning affairs of relatives and worldly things, and above all, talking that violates Charity.

3. Nobody is allowed to stay away without permission for trivial reasons.

4. Regular Recreations are from dinner to 1:30 P. M. and from 7 to 8 P. M.

5. Extra Recreations are granted not by the Sister Superior, but only by the Mother Superior.

§ 4. LETTERS.

1. The Sisters are not permitted to send Letters or to open them without having presented them to the Sister Superior for inspection. Letters directed to the Bishop or Mother Superior, or sent by them, are not sub-

ject to this rule; also the letters of ex-Mother Superiors, of the actual Assistants of the Mother Superior, and of the Mistress of Novices.

2. The letters of the Novices and of the Postulants are to pass through the hands of the Mistresses and be inspected by them, and may also be inspected by the Sister Superior.

3. Ordinarily speaking the Sisters are expected to write to their parents twice a year; the Novices may write three times.

§ 5. Enclosure.

1. The Sisters are not permitted to leave the Enclosure without permission of the Sister Superior; the Sister Superior ought to give this permission only in those cases that are specified by the Mother Superior for each House.

2. Without special permission of the Mother Superior who will grant it only on account of serious reasons the Sister Superior will not be absent from the House except in cases of pressing and open necessity, which admit no delay. In these cases however she must as soon as possible notify the Mother Superior, and state to her the reasons and the time of her absence.

3. The Mother Superior shall in case of necessity only permit Sisters to go abroad; and she herself, will only leave the House when the interests of the Community repuire it, as business that cannot be done by other persons demands it.

4. A reliable person ought to do the necessary buying and ordering articles.

5. The Sisters are forbidden to pay, under whatever

pretence, visits, or to be present at festivals, dinners, and suppers.

6. It is not a favorable sign for a Sister to nourish or express the desire to visit her parents or relatives; for on leaving the world she has sacrificed to God these inclinations. The Sisters ought therefore, to refuse every invitation that is made by their relatives, if they invite them solely for worldly motives.

7. When travelling, the Sister must go to those places only to which the Mother Superior sends them and look after those that are commissioned to them. They must also return at the time appointed by the Mother Superior.

8. Whenever a Sister even a Sister Superior remains on a journey longer in another House than two or three days, she will be under obedience of the Superior of that House.

9. In Houses where there is no Chapel, the Sisters assist at Divine Services in the Parochial Church.

10. In case strangers wish to see the Convent, they are shown only into the Chapel, garden, and those rooms that are occupied by the pupils. This must however, only be done with the permission of the Superior.

11. Entrance into the cells and into the infirmary is permitted to the Father Confessor and to the Physician. At the visits of the Physician, one Sister or the Superior, must always be present. In case the Father Confessor has to visit a sick Sister the Infirmarian will retire in such a way as not to lose sight of the infirm Sister, so as to be able to wait on her when needed.

12. The sewing room of the Sisters, the Refectory and the kitchen are also included in the Enclosure.

13. According to the rules of the Holy See, the Priests appointed to the Convent, as also the Servants and the laborers are not allowed to dwell in the Convent, and are permitted to converse with the Sisters and pupils only as far as their offices require it.

14. No Sister will be allowed to leave the Convent without a Sister or a pupil as a companion. The companion has to be appointed by the Sister Superior and is not to be elected by the Sister. In decorating altars in Parochial Churches, there must always be two Sisters together doing it; and it ought to be done, if possible when the faithful did not yet assemble. In case a Sister goes to Confession, another one will go along to the Church.

§ 6. CHAPEL.

The Mother Superior will endeavor to provide a proper Chapel for every Convent, where, with the necessary permission, the Blessed Sacrament will be kept.

§ 7. REFECTORY.

1. The Sisters will repair to the Refectory walking in a becoming gait, at the first signal of the bell. Those Sisters who arrive there too late will kneel down, kiss the floor, say one *Pater and Ave,* and kiss the floor again.

2. The Refectory must be large enough to accommodate all the Sisters.

3. There ought to be in the Refectory one Crucifix,

one Statute or Picture of the Blessed Virgin, and one of our holy Father St. Francis.

4. Tables and seats ought to be of common wood and all the other furniture for the use of the Sisters, of common materials.

5. One of the Sisters is to be appointed by the Sister Superior to be the Refectorian.

§ 8. Sewing Room.

1. The Sister who is appointed prefect in the sewing Room will take care of everything that is therein, and see that all is well done.

2. She moreover has to see that during hours of sewing the prayers are said and spiritual reading takes place, silence be kept and the holy Rule faithfully observed.

3. The sewing Room ought to be well arranged; the necessary cupboards, with drawers be there; also one crucifix and some religious pictures and books of devotion.

§ 9. Kitchen.

1. Without permission of the Sister Superior, none save the appointed Sisters are allowed to enter the kitchen.

2. Those Sisters that are appointed for the kitchen must endeavor to observe silence, be careful not to lose their temper and cheerfulness and must not be impolite towards those that ask at the shutter.

§ 10. Parlor.

1. No Sister is allowed to enter the Parlor without

permission of the Sister Superior. The Superior will, if possible send another Sister along.

2. The Sisters are never allowed to dine in the Parlor with strangers, not even with their relatives.

3. They will be very cautious in conversation with strangers and not appear inquisitive concerning the affairs of the world. In case worldly affairs from the topic of conversation, they ought prudently to direct it to edifying subjects.

4. In case the Sisters are flattered by outsiders, they ought not to answer, but act as if they had not understood it. They themselves must never indulge in flatteries, but must try to acquire earnestness, united with friendliness, in their dealings with outsiders.

5. They must never tell the Sisters, not even the Sister Superior, news of the world outside, which they heard from strangers, except such as are necessary to be known by the Superior, or as are apt to edify the Community.

6. The Sisters must struggle against the propensity to talkativeness and to impropriety; they must guard their senses as the doors to the soul and to the heart ought to be guarded. This is particularly true in regard to the eyes. They ought therefore, to practice great carefulness concerning them.

7. They are not allowed to speak to strangers nor to their relatives, nor to their pupils, about things concerning the holy Rule or the Customs of the Community.

8. Whenever an opportunity presents itself to speak

about other religious Communities, it will have to be done with great esteem and respect.

9. They must not intrude into the temporal affairs of strangers, not even into those of their relatives; for they have left the world and its cares, and selected God alone to be their portion and their inheritance.

10. As soon as the bell gives the signal for the religious exercises, they must politely beg to be excused and leave, provided urging reasons do not justify an exception.

11. The Parlors must be realy plain, even in those Convents with Academies. Nothing superfluous, nor costly furniture, should be seen therein. The doors leading into them must be so-called glass doors.

CHAPTER VII.

CARE FOR THE SICK.

1. In every Convent one of the Sisters is appointed Infirmarian, whose business it is to wait on the sick and suffering Sisters.

2. In the Infirmary she will keep everything in good order, and also in the cells of those Sisters who are not yet removed thither.

3. The Infirmarian ought to be altogether charity and kindness in attending the sick, well considering that she is, whilst serving them, serving our Divine Redeemer.

4. She must carefully listen to what the Physician directs, and punctually execute his prescriptions.

5. In as far as the state of the sick permits it, she

will assist them in saying Morning and Night Prayers, and in performing Spiritual Reading.

6. In case the Infirmarian has too much to do, the Superior will appoint one or more Sisters to wait, under the direction of the Infirmarian, on the infirm Sisters.

7. The Superiors must daily visit the seriously infirm Sisters and see that they have everything they need and that can ease them.

8. All the Sisters should truly sympathize with the suffering and infirm Sisters; readily visit them, with the Superior's permission; console them and perform for them some little acts of Charity. In visiting them they must not forget that the visits ought to be an edification and exortation to the infirm, but not a disturbance to their minds, by useless conversation.

9. The sick and the feeble Sisters must try to unite their suffering with the pangs of the suffering and expiring Redeemer.

10. The Sisters who are convalescent, as also those whose delicate constitutions make an exception to the usual Community life necessary; will remember that they always remain Members of a Community of Penance, and ought therefore, accept with a grateful heart whatever the Physician, or the charity of the Superiors of the Infirmarian presents.

They must particularly guard against the propensity to sensibility and commodity which may easily take possession of such persons; finally, they should joyfully greet the day on which they can again, with renewed strength and without exception, follow the common life.

11. In case a sick Sister thinks she has reasons to complain about the Infirmarian, she must be careful not to complain to other Sisters about her, but candidly and plainly explain herself to the Sisters Superior.

CHAPTER VIII.

§ 1. VISITATION BY ECCLESIASTICAL SUPERIORS.

1. Whenever it pleases the Bishop of the Diocese to perform the Canonical Visitation of a Convent or have it done by a Delegate, the Sister Superior and the Sisters are bound to respond, with candidness and plainness, to every question directed to them by his Lordship.

§ 2. VISITATION BY THE MOTHER SUPERIOR.

1. The Mother Superior should, at least once a year, perform the Visitation of the Houses to keep the fervor of religious life, awake and to preserve uniformity in the observance of the holy Rule and Constitutions. She will, at such a visit, call for all the Sisters of the House, that they may have an opportunity to reveal, without fear, their personal needs and the abuses that may have entered the House. At this occasion they must be careful to avoid harshness and exaggerations which easily dictate words that are not attending to truth.

2. The Mother Superior directs in the spirit of charity to every one the necessary exortations; she corrects, as far as she can, whatever needs correction; she confirms in exhorts every Sister to a virtuous life, as the calling of each may require it.

3. She ought to inquire at the Visitation whether

the Sisters and the other inmates of the House receive the necessary nourishment and care, and whether the works of charity, done by the House, are done well. She likewise examines whether the buildings are kept in good repair, and whether the possessions of the House are well administered. She investigates the treasury and the books, and sees whether the archives are kept in order.

4. In case the Mother Superior cannot personally make the Visitation on account of divers affairs or sickness, she will delegate one of her Assistants to this effect. This Sister must act in everything according to the orders of the Mother Superior, whose seat in the House she occupies during the whole time of the Visitation.

§ 3. Expulsion of Incorrigible Sisters.

1. In case a Sister (which God forbid) violates the vows griveously or causes continual scandal to the other Sisters by her irreligious Conduct, and, notwithstanding the repeated admonitions and threats given by the Superiors, does not amend, the Mother Superior's Council will entreat the Bishop of the Diocese to dispense the Sister (whose expulsion is deemed necessary) from her vows.

2. This petition, sent to the Bishop, must contain an exact statement of the faults of the Sister and of the means that were used to correct her.

She who is thus expelled from the Community can never be received again. Her dowry is returned, yet without interest. (This holds also good with those who have for good reasons obtained a dispensation from the Bishop.) In none of these two cases can the Sister that leaves the Community reclaim the alms or presents given by her, on her own accord, to the Community.

CHAPTER IX.

DUTIES TOWARDS THE DECEASED.

1. As soon as a Sister has departed this life, the Sister Superior will announce the death to all the Houses of the Community.

2. The Sister Superior will see that on the day of deposition a Solemn Requiem be celebrated, and that ten holy masses be said for the departed Sisters as soon as possible.

3. Every Sister who wore the habit longer than ten years will receive an additional mass for every year above ten years.

4. The Mother Superier, dying whilst she is in office, will receive one mass from every Mission House and three masses extra from the Mother House.

5. A Sister Superior will receive three Masses extra from the House where she departed Superior, and one extra from the Mother House.

6. Each Sister, will, within eight days after the notice of the death of a Sister was received, say fifty "Pater Noster" and "Requiem Æternam" after each "Pater Noster"; moreover, offer all her prayers, communions and good works, within these eight days for the same end.

7. The Sister Superior of every House orders one

holy mass to be said on All-Souls day, or within the Octave, for the Sisters departed.

8. Once a'month the Sisters say a part of the Office for the Dead, viz.: One Nocturn and the Lauds. On All-Souls day and five times during the year, the whole Office for the Dead is recited in the Mother-House. On these six days there is a Requiem Mass said in the Mother House to the following intentions.

1st. Nov. 2nd: for the faithful departed in general.

2d. In February: for the deceased Sisters friends end benefactors.

3d. In July: for the deceased Sisters, friends and benefactors.

4th. In September; for the deceased Sisters, friends and benefactors.

5th. In November: for the deceased Parents of the Sisters.

6th. In December: for the departed members of the three Orders, and for their parents, friends and benefactors, and for all those that in any way belonged to the three Orders, or that rest in their Churches.

Besides this, every Sister says, in the course of the year, one hundred Pater and Requiem for the departed in general.

APPENDIX.

1. Order of the Day: The Sisters will arise at 4½ A. M., retire at 9 P. M., and, as punctually as possible, comply with the respective Order of the Day.

2. The Blessing and the Curse of St. Francis and the holy Rule must be read every Friday, except on

Festivals, and these Constitutions twice every year, viz.,
in the Months of January and August.

   3. Order to be observed in the Community.

   1. Mother Superior, actual.

   2. Sister Superior, i. e., Local Superior, when her
Community is present.

   3. Ex-Mothers, according to their ages in the Community.

   4. Assistants to Mother Superior.

   5. Mistress of Novices.

   6. Sisters Superiors of the Mission Houses, according to their ages.

   7. The other Sisters according to their ages, i. e.,
from the day they received the Habit.

   8. Novices, according to their ages.

   9. Postulants.

CHAPTER X.

OBLIGATION CONTAINED IN THE HOLY RULE AND IN THESE CONSTITUTIONS.

   1. Our holy Church, this dearly loving Mother, approved the Rule of the Third Order. She trusted, when
approving it, that the intimate love towards the crucified Redeemer would alone induce all the members of
said Order to observe it faithfully. For St. Francis,
our dear Father, left to all children this beautiful inheritance.

   The ardent love towards Christ crucified. We should
therefore imitate him, and perfect daily the sacrifice we
offered when making the Vows. The Church considers
it therefore superfluous to command that the Rule be

observed under pain of sin. She declares the Rule of the Third Order not binding under mortal or venial sin. The same is to be said about these Constitutions.

2. The Sisters will consequently, understand it well, (but they shall not say on account of this declaration, "I do not care; they do not oblige under sin") they should serve God more faithfully and observe them with a strict fidelity, out of love. They should esteem it a happiness to be able to gain great merits before God by observing the smallest Rule faithfully, without being obliged, under pain of sin, to do so.

3. They will likewise esteem themselves happy, considering themselves bound to strive after perfection to have found in the holy Rule a sure and easy way to save their souls and to attain sanctity. They must stir up their fervor at the thought that so many Saints of both sexes entered eternal bliss by faithfully observing the holy Rule of the Third Order.

4. The Sisters are nevertheless obliged, in virtue of their Vows, to observe during their whole life, Poverty, Chastity and Obedience. In transgressing these Vows, they would become guilty of a sacrilege before God; and as the Sisters bound themselves at their profession to lead a life according to the Rule and these Constitutions, they must have the permanent will to observe both.

A Sister who would have the contrary will or (which God forbid) would formally contemn the holy Rule, these Constitutions, or the Authority of the Superiors, could sin mortally before God.

5. It is the intention of our Holy Mother, the Church, the wish of our Holy Father, St. Francis, that we should keep our holy Rules for the love of God, aiming at a perfection ever increasing, retaining at the same time full peace of conscience.

But to violate the Rules out of contempt is a sign of great levity and laxity, not consistent with a truly religious life,—and consequently cannot be done without sins contrary to the great duty of all Religions, viz.: to aim at Christian perfection. It is, therefore, easily understood--and experience testifies it--that such careless Religions deprive themselves, more and more, of God's graces and sometimes even so far as to lose the very grace of their holy vocation.

6. Moreover, such transgressions, repeatedly committed are doing a great deal of harm to the whole Community, by relaxing religious life and good discipline, by giving scandal not only to Religions, but also to seculars, thus impeding the good and edifying exampel the Community should give to the world.

7. As this Community professes the Rule, approved by His Holiness Leo X., the Sisters can gain all the indulgences, either personal or local that are granted to the three Orders of St. Francis.

8. The Superiors are bound, in conscience, to lead the Sisters, by word and example, to observe faithfully the holy Rule and these Constitutions; they must try to guard religious discipline by constant vigilance; prevent faults, if possible; punish transgressions with prudence and charity.

9. The Superiors are responsible to God for all these duties. They are bound to give an account not only of their own conduct, but also of that of the Sisters whom they had to lead on to perfection and whose faults they could and should have prevented.

10. Every Sister, therefore, will endeavor to sanctify herself and her fellow Sisters through faithful observance of the holy Rule and of the Constitutions; she will continually seek to lighten the burden pressing so heavily on the Superiors. The Community will thus be to each Sister the entrance into Heaven; and those who were united here on earth in the service of God will also in eternity be united inseperably in the choir of Virgins who always follow the Lamb whithersoever He goeth. Apoc. XIV., 4.

www.ingramcontent.com/pod-product-compliance
Lightning Source LLC
Chambersburg PA
CBHW031751090426
42739CB00008B/960